A BICYCLE FOR ROSAURA

This edition is published by special arrangement with Kane/Miller
Book Publishers.

Grateful acknowledgment is made to Kane/Miller Book Publishers for
permission to reprint *A Bicycle for Rosaura* by Daniel Barbot, illustrated by
Morella Fuenmayor. Copyright © 1990 by Ediciones Ekaré-Banco del Libro.
First published in the United States by Kane/Miller Book Publishers, 1991.

Printed in Mexico

ISBN 0-15-302140-3

4 5 6 7 8 9 10 050 97 96 95

A BICYCLE FOR ROSAURA

Daniel Barbot

Illustrated by Morella Fuenmayor

HARCOURT BRACE & COMPANY

Orlando   Atlanta   Austin   Boston   San Francisco   Chicago   Dallas   New York
Toronto   London

Señora Amelia loved animals. At
home she had a dog, a kitten, a talking
parrot, a turtle, twin canaries and a
handsome hen named Rosaura.

The month before Rosaura's birthday, Señora Amelia asked, "Have you decided what you'd like for your birthday?"

"Why, yes. A bicycle!" said Rosaura.

"But that's impossible!" Señora Amelia exclaimed. "Who's ever heard of a hen riding a bicycle?"

"That's just it," Rosaura replied. "I want to be the first!"

Señora Amelia wanted to please her hen.

"Tomorrow I will try to find a bicycle for Rosaura," she decided.

Early the next morning she took the bus into the city and stopped in all the bicycle shops. In each and every one she got the same response.

"What? A bicycle for a hen?"

Or, "No way. We don't carry any such model."

Or, "Let's take a look in the catalog. Sorry, señora. They don't make bikes for hens."

So Señora Amelia went home sad and disappointed.

"Rosaura is going to be awfully upset if I have to tell her that I couldn't find her a bicycle," she thought.

As the days passed, Señora Amelia began to think that it *was* hopeless.

Then, one afternoon a strange-looking man came into town. He walked up and down the streets singing and calling:

"I mend old clocks and jack-in-the-boxes.
I repair harmonicas and wind-chimes.
I sharpen penknives and sewing scissors.
I make rollerskates for dogs and eyeglasses for cats."

"Maybe that man can help me," thought Señora Amelia.
And she called him over right away.

"What can I do for you señora?" asked the man. "Would you like a singing spoon, a lunar calendar, a chocolate rocking chair . . . . ?"

"No, no," interrupted Señora Amelia. "What I need is . . . a bicycle for my hen."

"Umm . . . Hmmm," murmured the man. "That is a difficult order. I'll have to take measurements. I need to know the length of her legs and the span of her wings."

After jotting down numbers and working out complicated formulas, the man was pleased to announce that he could have the bicycle finished in time for Rosaura's birthday.

The days seemed endless.

Finally, one morning there was a knock at her door. Señora Amelia peeked outside . . . and saw the wonderful bicycle for Rosaura!

She wrapped it up in a big box, tied a bright red ribbon around it, and on the day of Rosaura's birthday . . .

Well, Rosaura was delighted with her present. Now, every morning she rides to the grocery store to buy milk and bread for Señora Amelia.

So, if you should ever visit this town in Venezuela, you're sure to see Rosaura speeding by on her bicycle. But . . . watch out! The strange man forgot the brakes!